WHERE'D THIS BOOK COME FROM?

Fancy Word: ⟶ Provenance

The word **provenance** means where something comes from, or its source.
Every record at the National Archives has a source. So does this book.

The provenance of this book began with the <u>New York Life Foundation</u>, who made a gift to the <u>Foundation for the National Archives</u> to hire a very talented group of artists and writers at <u>FableVision</u> to work alongside the very talented curators and educators of the <u>National Archives Experience</u> to tell the story of the <u>National Archives.</u>

So Thora and Peter and Paul and Lee Ann and Marvin and Christina and Shelby and Karen and Will and Bob and Edda and Renee and Carol and Loren sat down to think about how to let you discover what really goes on at the National Archives.

And we crammed a lot of great pictures and maps and letters and activities into this book, but we left just enough room for you to make it your own.

Now that the book is in YOUR hands, you've become part of the provenance pass-along-party — so add YOUR name and info to document it officially!

Name: . . . .

Address: . . . .

. . . .

How I got this book: . . . .

. . . .

Date: . . . .

 FOUNDATION FOR THE NATIONAL ARCHIVES

 FableVision

 NEW YORK LIFE

 If you meet these guys, thank them for helping make this book possible!

1

What DOES the National Archives do?

As an Archivist-in-Training, you'll be asked this at fancy parties, by curious reporters, and at random bus stops. Okay — here's the scoop — and **this part is REALLY REALLY important**:

The National Archives is here to "keep it real" — to collect the evidence that tells the TRUE story of who we are as a free nation. It's all here — the good, the bad, and the ugly — even the stuff that shows our government made mistakes. **Because democracy needs the truth.**

And to "Keep it Real"...

The National Archives holds the records — TONS of 'em (literally) — of our Federal Government. We have records documenting the rights of citizens, the actions of government officials, and the "national experience" (a.k.a. the Whole American Story).

And to document all that means keeping BILLIONS of:

- **documents**
- **photographs**
- **maps**
- **posters**
- **architectural drawings**
- **audio recordings**
- **motion picture films and videos**
- **electronic records and more!**

In short, a LOT of stuff!
And we are still growing!

A billion is a thousand millions!

There are some pretty famous documents...

Supreme Court of the United States

No. 1 —— , October Term, 19 54

Oliver Brown, Mrs. Richard Lawton, Mrs. Sadie Emmanuel et al.

Appellants,

vs.

Board of Education of Topeka, Shawnee County, Kansas, et al.

Appeal from the United States District Court for the —————————— District of Kansas.

This cause came on to be heard on the transcript of the record from the United States District Court for the —————————— District of Kansas, —————————— and was argued by counsel.

This is the Supreme Court judgment in the case *Brown v. Board of Education* that ended legal segregation in United States schools. Before this, public schools could teach white and black children separately. This document says that segregation is illegal under the Constitution — a major turning point in the civil rights movement.

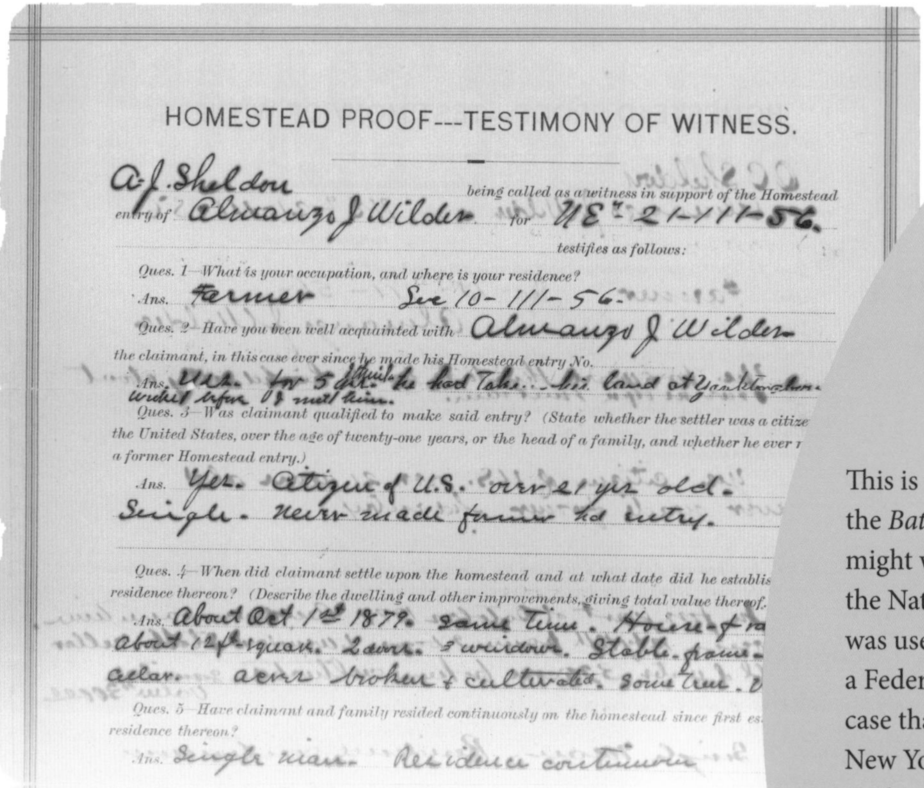

HOMESTEAD PROOF---TESTIMONY OF WITNESS.

[handwritten homestead proof document]

A. J. Sheldon being called as a witness in support of the Homestead entry of Almanzo J. Wilder for NE¼ 21-111-56.

testifies as follows:

Ques. 1—What is your occupation, and where is your residence?
Ans. Farmer   Sec 10-111-56.

Ques. 2—Have you been well acquainted with Almanzo J Wilder the claimant, in this case ever since he made his Homestead entry No.
Ans. Yes. for 5 years— he had taken his land at Yankton when before I met him.

Ques. 3—Was claimant qualified to make said entry? (State whether the settler was a citizen of the United States, over the age of twenty-one years, or the head of a family, and whether he ever made a former Homestead entry.)
Ans. Yes. Citizen of U.S. over 21 yrs old. Single. Never made former had entry.

Ques. 4—When did claimant settle upon the homestead and at what date did he establish residence thereon? (Describe the dwelling and other improvements, giving total value thereof.)
Ans. About Oct 1st 1879. same time. House of ... about 12ft square. 2 doors. 2 windows. Stable. frame ... celar. acres broken & cultivated. some time. ...

Ques. 5—Have claimant and family resided continuously on the homestead since first establishing residence thereon?
Ans. Single man.   Residence continuous.

Ques. 6—For what period or periods has the settler been absent from the land since making ..., and for what purpose, and if temporarily absent, did claimant's family reside upon and ...

There's the real personal stuff…

This is Almanzo Wilder's application to become owner of 160 acres in South Dakota. Under the Homestead Act of 1862, if he lived and worked the land for five years, he could own it. You may have heard of Almanzo's wife. Her name was Laura Ingalls…Wilder. She wrote books for children about pioneer life. Some of those stories became the television show "Little House on the Prairie."

There's also the surprising stuff…

This is the first issue of the *Batman* comic. You might wonder why it is in the National Archives. It was used as evidence in a Federal District Court case that took place in New York. The National Archives has all sorts of records and objects that were submitted as evidence in Federal court cases.

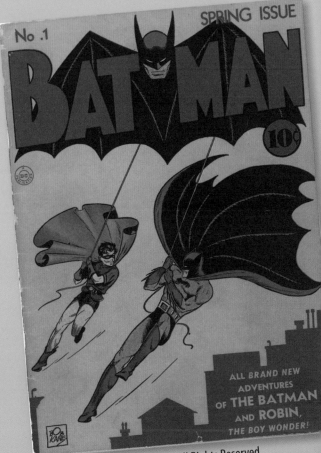

The National Archives Building in Washington, DC, is BIG — it occupies two full city blocks…

OPEN THE DOORS and LET'EM IN!

The National Archives doesn't just lock all the stuff away.
We make the government's records available for the people TO USE!

More than 95% of the National Archives' records are open for research...

AND all kinds of people use them — filmmakers, students, lawyers, software developers, journalists, authors, genealogists, and many, many others. Including YOU now!

In the mountains of records, there are clues to who this nation is, where our people came from, what worked and didn't work as we all built this great country together. As an Archivist-in-Training, you're now part of the team discovering stories that matter.

Knowing **what** happened —
and **how** it happened —
gives people the **power** to decide
what to do **now** and in the **future.**

"This building holds in trust the records of our national life and symbolizes our faith in the permanency of our national institutions."

— from an inscription on the east side of the National Archives Building

WOW! You hear President Theodore Roosevelt "waxing on" at the turn of the 20th century!

Wax cylinders are the earliest form of sound recordings in the National Archives. People can still hear these historical recordings, thanks to audio technicians in the National Archives laboratories. They make copies using equipment specifically designed to play these cylinders.

4

...and the National Archives at College Park, Maryland, is even bigger!

ALL OF A SUDDEN...

OH NO!! IT'S THE GIANT TERMITES FROM OUTER SPACE!

AHHHHHHH!

DON'T PANIC! WE CAN MAKE IT! JUST STAY IN LINE--

JUST STAY IN LINE. ONE AT A TIME! YOU'LL ALL GET IN.

UGH! COULD THIS BE ANY MORE BORING? WHAT A WASTE OF TIME.

WHAT ARE YOU TALKING ABOUT? I CAN'T WAIT TO GET INTO THE NATIONAL ARCHIVES!

THINK OF ALL THE RECORDS WE'LL SEE! I'M AN ARCHIVIST-IN-TRAINING, YOU KNOW.

WHY WOULD ANYONE WANT TO BE AN ARCHIVIST IN ANYTHING?

I THINK THE ROTUNDA IS UP AHEAD! EEEEE! THIS IS SO EXCITING!

WHY DO THEY KEEP ALL THIS OLD STUFF? AND WHY DO WE HAVE TO LOOK AT IT?

PUBLIC VAULTS

THIS IS THE REAL STUFF! THESE ARE THE PAPERS PEOPLE WROTE ON. IT'S FANTASTIC TO SEE THEM, IN PERSON!

WOW! ISN'T THIS AMAZING?

BUT WHO CARES? WHAT'S THIS GOT TO DO WITH ME?

BEN

YOU DON'T GET IT! THESE THINGS CONNECT US TO OUR PAST.

SO WHAT? IT'S IN THE PAST.

WELL, KNOWING WHAT HAPPENED CAN HELP US MAKE DECISIONS IN THE FUTURE.

I JUST NEED TO DECIDE WHAT I WANT FOR LUNCH!

BEN

WHERE ARE WE?

HOW DID WE GET HERE?

WAIT, ARE THESE THE REAL STACKS? THE ACTUAL RECORDS?

WHO CARES?!! HOW DID WE GET HERE, AND HOW DO WE GET BACK?

I DON'T WANT TO MISS LUNCH!

HI THERE! I'M BEN FRANKLIN.

YOU KNOW...THE INVENTOR, JOURNALIST, AND STATESMAN? I'VE DONE A LOT OF THINGS. BUT TODAY, I'M HERE TO HELP YOU APPRECIATE THE NATIONAL ARCHIVES.

LOOK, BUDDY...WE NEED TO GET BACK TO OUR GROUP. IT'S LUNCH TIME, AND OUR TEACHERS ARE GONNA HAVE A COW IF THEY FIND OUT WE'RE MISSING.

YEAH, MR. PINKERT WILL KILL US.

YOU WON'T BE MISSED JUST YET. RIGHT NOW, YOU NEED TO UNDERSTAND THAT EVERYONE HAS A CONNECTION TO THE RECORDS IN THE NATIONAL ARCHIVES. WE'RE GOING ON A FIELD TRIP OF OUR OWN.

WATCH THIS!

TO BE CONTINUED...

7

Cool Stuff

This is just a sampling of some of the cool stuff we've collected at the National Archives. There are all sorts of stories in these records. Check them out!

NASA-CFD TAPE No. T-0
(REEL #2)

8:31

Buzz Aldrin was photographed on the moon, and during an earlier mission the crew of *Apollo 8* was interviewed on television. From space!

of what he's seen today. I know my
is that it's a vast, lonely forbidding type
se of nothing, that looks rather like clouds
pumice stone, and it certainly would not appe
iting place to live or work. Ji
st about.

Well, Frank, my thoug
liness up here of the moon i
realize just what you have b
here is a grand ovation t

Bill, what do you th
I think the thing th
nar's sunrises and sunset
stark nature of the terrai
ly bring out the relief that i
s very bri

APE.

Scientific American
MUNN & Co
AMERICAN & FOREIGN
PATENT ATTORNEYS
OFFICES
37 PARK ROW & 145 NASSAU ST
NEW YORK.

No. 96208

C.E. Dayton's Velocipede.

Fig.1

The velocipede was an early bicycle. This patent application details a new gear system. Every part of every invention must be described to receive a patent.

ADDRESSES

ADDRESSE

Name
Str
Cit
Pho
Name
Phone 642 - 599
Name

This tape recorder, address book, and letter of resignation were all connected to the Watergate scandal in the Nixon administration.

UNIVERSAL
567
UHER

EXHIBIT
MISC 47-78

Dear Mr. Secretary:

I hereby resign the Office of President of the United States.

Sincerely,

Name
Street
City

PIGEON MESSAGE

RECEIVED AT MESSAGE CENTER ~~MESSAGE~~ 4:22 PM

TO C. O. 308th INFANTRY

FROM 1st BN 308th INFANTRY

        WE ARE ALONG THE ROAD PARALELL 276.4. OUR ARTILLERY IS DROPPING
A BARRAGE DIRECTLY ON US. FOR HEAVENS SAKE STOP IT.

                                    WHITTLESAY
                                    MAJ 308th

BIRD RELEASED 3 P.M.

RECEIVED AT LOFT 4:05
DISTRIBUTION
G 3

This message was sent from behind enemy lines during WWI. It was carried by a pigeon.

Men Wanted for the Army

These two Army recruiting posters are about 80 years apart in age.

This is Captain Andrew B. Turner, a pilot in WWII. He was part of the Tuskegee Airmen.

[RETURN TO BE MADE TO POST SUPERINTENDENT.]

Fort Pickering Tenn March 25 1865.

...VE this day united in Matrimony. *Reuben Woods* of *Fort Pickering Tenn* and
...ncy *Woods* of *Memphis Tenn* Age of man 52 years; color. *Black* do. of his
Black do. of his mother, *Black* lived with another woman 2 years; separated from her by
...ing *Sold*. Age of woman, 27 years; color, *Brown* do. of her father, *Black* do. of her mother,
...pper lived with another man 1 years; separated from him by *being Sold*. They, unitedly, have
...1 children; do. of the man by previous connection, 1 ; do. of the woman by do. 2 .

...NESS: *Henry Woods*

Anthony Arnold

This certificate records the marriage of two former slaves.

WHAT SOME OF THE MOST SUCCESSFUL WOMEN ARE WEARING THIS YEAR.

ARMY. BE ALL YOU CAN BE.

9

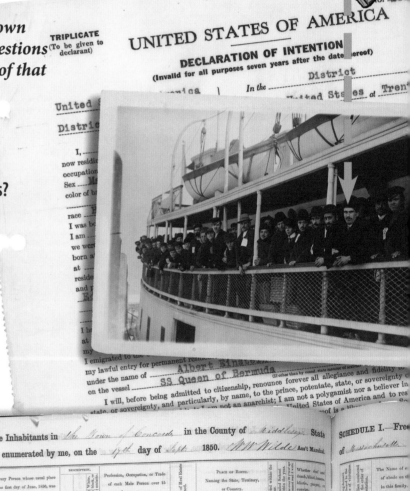

Before you go any further in your AiT training, let's turn the focus on...you.

ARCHIVE THIS: YOU!

As an Archivist-in-Training, you should document your own story — and your family's story. Answer the following questions — and back each up with some "hold-in-your-hand" proof that each answer is true.

- **When and where you were born?**

- **Who are some important family members? What are their names?**

- **Where does your family come from?**

- **Where do you live? Where else have you lived?**

- **What are some important stories from your family history?**

What documents, photos, videos, and sound recordings do you have — or do you know about — that can help you answer these questions? You can use this checklist to "get archived"!

CHECKLIST:

- ☐ Photo of yourself or family members
- ☐ Copy of your birth certificate
- ☐ Your library card
- ☐ Your school ID
- ☐ Your social security card
- ☐ A written or recorded story about your family
- ☐ A documented story about your birth or the birth of someone else in your family
- ☐ Copy of a map showing your present home, or past homes, or even other regions of the country or world where your family has lived
- ☐ Mail showing your present address or a past address
- ☐ List of family members. How far back can you go with certainty?

Who Are

Find a family that may have recently immigrated to the United States. Is anyone in your family a recent immigrant?

Find a family that shows many generations. How many generations of your family lived in America?

Find a family that worked the land. Has anyone in your family worked on a farm?

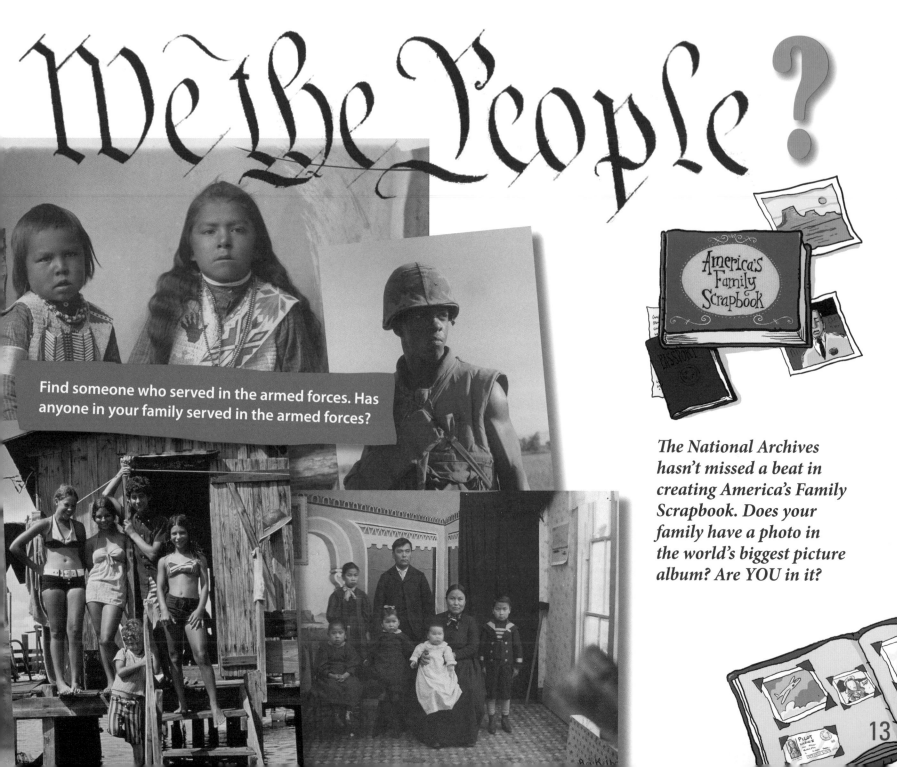

We the People?

Find someone who served in the armed forces. Has anyone in your family served in the armed forces?

The National Archives hasn't missed a beat in creating America's Family Scrapbook. Does your family have a photo in the world's biggest picture album? Are YOU in it?

America's Family Scrapbook

13

Drum roll please...the next four documents are the "mega-stars" of the National Archives. As an AiT member, this is "gotta know" material!

Declaration of Independence

Imagine starting a revolution by writing on a piece of animal skin! The American colonists did just that with this declaration to Great Britain: Sorry, King George, you're outta here! We've got a democracy to invent.

Want to see it up close and personal? The Declaration on view in the National Archives is THE official engrossed copy. It was written with a quill pen and iron gall ink on parchment (not paper).

This copy of the Declaration has gotten around. It traveled to Philadelphia, Lancaster, and York, all in Pennsylvania. It went to Princeton and Trenton, New Jersey. It even moved between Baltimore and Annapolis, Maryland, and New York City — all before 1800!

During certain wars it was moved to a safe location. It has been stored and displayed in several places in Washington, DC. Since 1952 its home has been the National Archives. Here, it is protected and on display, for everyone to see.

• *Engrossing* is how important copies were made before printers and copiers. "Engross" comes from a word that means to "make big" — and people wanted the big deal documents to be easy to read. So, an *engrossed copy* was written with large characters.

• *Parchment* looks like paper, which is made from plants. But parchment is generally made from the skin of a sheep or goat. The hair is removed, and the skin is rubbed smooth and then made very thin. That's what our country's earliest important documents are written on.

• *Iron gall ink* is made by mixing iron sulfate, gum, water and galls. Galls are abnormal plant growths caused by an organism, usually a small insect. Iron gall ink was used as long ago as 2500 BC. The Dead Sea Scrolls were written with it. Da Vinci, Bach, and Rembrandt used it. Some European countries required legal documents to be written with it. It doesn't rub off parchment like other inks do. Lucky for us!

Constitution

This famous "We the People" document is the mission-critical "blueprint" that set up our three branches of government — and it's been working nonstop for centuries. It's not often you'll find something that lasts so long with very few tune ups!

About 70 years ago, a long and careful search of public documents revealed that Jacob Shallus was the mystery penman who created the document now on display in the National Archives.

At the time of the Constitutional Convention, Jacob Shallus was assistant clerk of the Pennsylvania State Assembly. His office was in the same building in which the Constitutional Convention was held.

There is a good chance that he never realized what a big deal the Constitution was. Today, of course, we know this amazing document has kept us on track for over two centuries. And it keeps going and going. **No wonder over a million** citizens and international visitors come see it every year!

The original signed Constitution is written on four pieces of parchment.

Bill of Rights

This document is your freedom blueprint — it lays out your rights as a U.S. citizen. Thank your lucky stars (and stripes) that it exists — it gives you rights that people in some countries can still only dream about!

The **Bill of Rights** in the National Archives is the *official* copy. It was approved by Congress and engrossed on parchment. On this copy are the twelve amendments that were sent to the states for their approval. But only ten amendments were ratified.

Strangely enough, practically nothing is known about where this copy of the Bill of Rights was kept between 1789 and 1938. That's 149 years! All that is known is that it was kept with other signed original laws and resolutions and moved with the government.

In 1938 it was one of many original documents transferred from the State Department to the National Archives.

This document has also had a public life. From September 1947 to January 1949, the Bill of Rights was the starring document on a tour of the **Freedom Train.** This train carried 126 historic documents to 322 cities. And today it's on permanent display with the **Declaration of Independence** and the **Constitution.** This one is also a "must see"!

• The Big Three — the *Declaration of Independence*, the *Constitution*, and the *Bill of Rights* — are called the *Charters of Freedom.*

• The Charters have been on public display at the National Archives Building since 1952.

For tons more info on the Declaration, Constitution, and Bill of Rights visit www.archives.gov.

Emancipation Proclamation

Nearly a century after the Charters of Freedom, the Emancipation Proclamation took a big step in booting slavery out of the United States. America's idea of freedom was growing and expanding to include EVERYONE.

The Emancipation Proclamation in the National Archives is the official document. Originally, the five-page document was tied with narrow red and blue ribbons, attached to the signature page by an impression of the seal of the United States. Parts of the seal have worn off, but most of the ribbon is still there.

President Abraham Lincoln signed the Emancipation Proclamation during the Civil War, on January 1, 1863, and it went into effect the moment he did so.

Even though it was a very important document, the signing was done quietly, late in the afternoon, in the President's study. There was no formal ceremony, and only a few friends were there.

When Lincoln picked up a pen to sign the Emancipation Proclamation, his arm shook. Then he remembered he had been greeting visitors to the White House all morning and had shaken hands for hours. He realized his arm was tired from all of that handshaking. But sign it he did — saying, "I never, in my life, felt more certain that I was doing right than I do in signing this paper." Go, Abe!

Slavery was finally abolished with the Thirteenth Amendment.

PUTTING THE PIECES TOGETHER

The United States was built on the "installment plan" — over two centuries. And the National Archives can tell you how and when it all happened!

The U.S. was cobbled together with treaties and other agreements over many decades — and we're just showing you some of them here. Rome wasn't built in a day — and neither was our nation. So, take some time — and get familiar with the installment plan. You get extra AiT member points for learning all this!

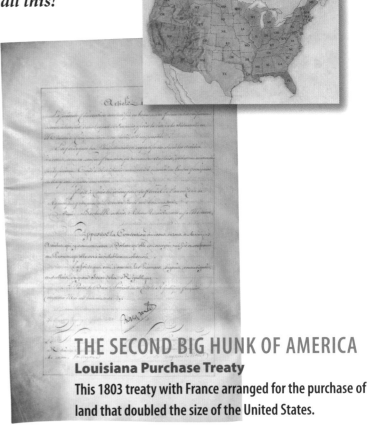

A GREAT START!
Treaty of Paris
This treaty ended the Revolutionary War. In signing it, England accepted American independence.

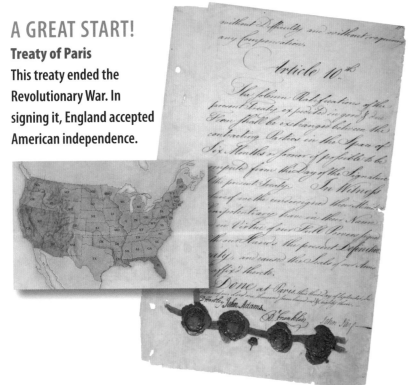

THE SECOND BIG HUNK OF AMERICA
Louisiana Purchase Treaty
This 1803 treaty with France arranged for the purchase of land that doubled the size of the United States.

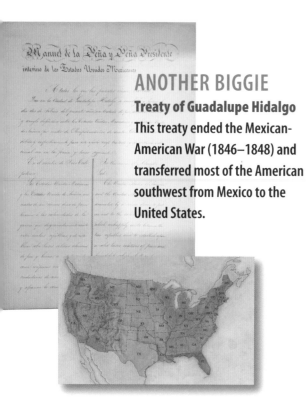

ANOTHER BIGGIE
Treaty of Guadalupe Hidalgo
This treaty ended the Mexican-American War (1846–1848) and transferred most of the American southwest from Mexico to the United States.

RUSHIN' TO OWN ALASKA
Alaska Check
With this check for $7.2 million to Russia in 1867, the United States bought 600,000 square miles, which became the territory and then the state of Alaska.

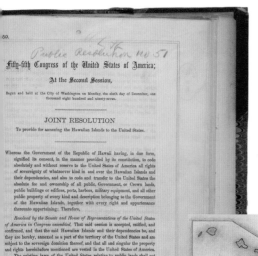

LET'S ADD HAWAII, TOO!
Hawaiian Annexation
For most of the 1800s, the U.S. and some European nations wanted to control Hawaii. Finally, in 1898, the U.S. annexed Hawaii.

So…
WHERE are you?

Depending on where you live, one of these documents may have made a big difference in your community. Is your home or school on land that became part of the United States because of one of these documents, or another? Jot down here where you live, what document(s) defined your community, and what might have been different if that document hadn't been signed:

HERE WE ARE. YOU MIGHT BE SURPRISED BY SOME OF OUR RECORDS.

WHO'S THAT LITTLE GUY?

POP!

I'M IN THE UNITED STATES AIR FORCE. I WORK ON PROJECT BLUE BOOK-- THAT'S THE INVESTIGATION OF UNIDENTIFIED FLYING OBJECTS. WE CALL 'EM UFOS!

HERE'S ONE OF OUR REPORTS. IT SHOWS THE MOST RECENT SIGHTINGS BETWEEN JUNE AND SEPTEMBER OF 1952. WE CORRELATED THE SIGHTINGS WITH STORIES ABOUT UFOS IN MAGAZINES.

ZIP!

UFOS? WOW! WHERE DID THAT GUY COME FROM? HOW DO YOU DO THAT?

I HAVE A CERTAIN CONNECTION TO THE ARCHIVES.

I'VE HEARD OF PROJECT BLUE BOOK. THEY INVESTIGATED UFOS FOR OVER 20 YEARS. CAN ANYONE READ THOSE REPORTS?

ABSOLUTELY! THE RECORDS ARE HERE FOR EVERYONE TO USE.

OKAY, SO YOU HAVE STUFF ABOUT UFOS. I STILL THINK 99 PERCENT OF WHAT'S HERE IS BORING.

YOU NEED MORE?

HERE WE GO AGAIN.

UMM... WHERE ARE WE NOW?

WHAT'S THIS, A DRAWING?

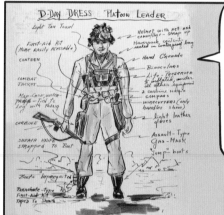

D-DAY DRESS PLATOON LEADER

THAT'S RIGHT! I'M A DRAWING OF WHAT PLATOON LEADERS ARE WEARING FOR THE D-DAY LANDING IN NORMANDY. THEY'LL HAVE TO START AN ATTACK AT SEA AND END IT ON LAND-- GETTING SHOT AT THE WHOLE TIME. I WAS DRAWN BY A COMBAT HISTORIAN, AND I GUESS HE THINKS THIS IS AN IMPORTANT EVENT.

IMPORTANT EVENT?! I'D SAY SO. THE D-DAY LANDING IN NORMANDY CHANGED THE COURSE OF WORLD WAR II!

THIS LOOKS FAMILIAR. IT LOOKS LIKE THE SOLDIERS IN A MOVIE I SAW LAST WEEK.

FILMMAKERS SOMETIMES USE OUR RECORDS TO MAKE THEIR STORIES MORE ACCURATE. THE INFORMATION USED IN THAT MOVIE MIGHT HAVE COME DIRECTLY FROM HERE.

FILMMAKERS?! HERE? WOW!

MANY DIFFERENT PEOPLE USE THE NATIONAL ACRHIVES-- YOU'D BE SURPRISED.

STILL, MOST OF THIS STUFF IS NOT ALL THAT INTERESTING. NOT TO REGULAR PEOPLE LIKE ME.

HMMM, WE'LL SEE ABOUT THAT.

ARE YOU GOING TO MAKE SOMEONE ELSE APPEAR? HOW ARE YOU DOING THIS?

HERE, WHY DON'T YOU GIVE IT A TRY.

TO BE CONTINUED...

:CLICK:

What do WE Keep and Why?

The National Archives cannot keep all of the thousands of records produced by the government every day. So how do we decide what to keep?

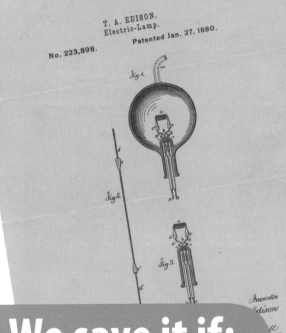

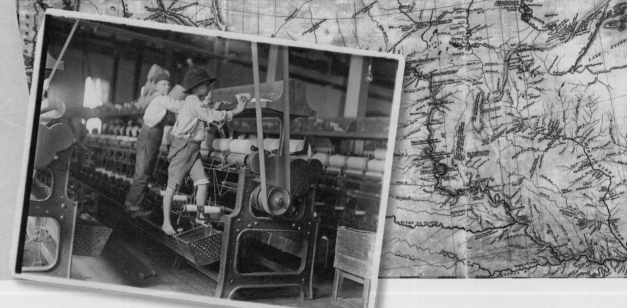

We save it if:

It documents the national experience

Some examples:

- **Patent drawings**
- **Film of the space shuttle explosion**
- **Combat photography**

It documents the rights of citizens

Some examples:

- **Claims of 9/11 victims**
- **Child labor investigations**
- **Treaties**

It documents the actions of Federal officials

Some examples:

- **FBI files**
- **Coast Guard rescue reports**
- **Official reports from explorers**

What do **YOU** Keep and Why?

Check out the places you and your family store records—a drawer, a locker, a wallet, a computer, a backpack, a closet, a box in the attic.

What records do you keep?
Why do you keep them?

Are they important to you? To your family? To some future need you don't know yet? Do you keep these records because they are significant? Because they are fun? Because they show or prove something?

Do you have any records that connect you to the Federal Government? (Like tax forms or a passport?)

As an Archivist-in-Training, you need to start working with records. So list some records you're keeping, and why. Ask your parents where important records are kept and see if they are being stored safely. You may want to work as a family to scan them for your own Family Digital Archives! Make sure you have a back-up....

the record	where we keep it	why we keep it

REMEMBER, records can include papers, computer files, photographs, maps, audio recordings, digital images, and more!

23

BEFORE THE NATIONAL ARCHIVES

Before 1934 government agencies stored their own records. While some took good care of their materials, some had no clue about protecting things the right way. Records were stored wherever there was room. Some records were disorganized, and some were stored carelessly. Fire, insects, heat, water, and/or sunlight damaged some records. That's enough to make any Archivist shake in his or her boots.

Yikes!

Here's what one storage area looked like.

HERE'S HOW WE KEEP RECORDS NOW

Now we've got it down. The National Archives keeps records in acid-free folders and boxes. We control temperature, humidity, and light. Storage rooms (we call them stack areas) are secure and fireproof. This is extreme archiving at its best!

Take note, oh fearless AiT — we also label all the records and keep track of where things are stored. Archivists write brief summaries of what is in each record series, along with notes (called "finding aids") to help locate them. Keeping our country's records has come a long way since 1934!

So, **ARCHIVIST-IN-TRAINING** Where are YOUR important records kept? Are the materials organized? Easy to find? Protected from possible damage? Start your personal, family, school or youth group archiving plan TODAY!

25

NOW WHAT?

So We've Saved All This Stuff…What Do People Do With It?

At the National Archives, the stuff we save is for people to USE. Ninety-five percent of all the materials we hold are available for people to use. (And remember: 95% of billions of records is A LOT of stuff!) Part of the National Archives mission is making sure that citizens have access to these records. How many countries can say that?

THE NATIONAL ARCHIVES HOLDS THE RECORDS OF THE NATION.

The existence of those records assures our rights as citizens; tells us what actually happened; helps us understand our past and ourselves. But the records only do this when they are used.

People use the National Archives for all kinds of reasons: To search. To compare. To think about. To prove. To understand. To tell stories. And to:

- discover family history
- track changes in a technology or business
- identify changes in a community
- change a law
- bring forgotten events to public knowledge
- hold the government accountable
- make a movie
- write a newspaper story
- write a history book
- hear recordings of White House conversations
- see footage of an event
- remember
- teach…

Where might **YOU** show up in the National Archives someday?

How cool would it be to have something you did or created end up being part of the National Archives? Now THAT'S a legacy. As an AiT Member, you should put that on your "life goals" list!

Maybe you'll end up in the National Archives...

- With a patent for an invention
- In a photo of an event
- As a name on a census record
- In an audio recording
- As a member of the armed forces
- In a letter to someone
- As an astronaut

- As President of the United States
- As a park ranger
- As a computer scientist
- As a marine biologist
- As a test pilot
- As a diplomat
- As an archivist

The possibilities are endless!

HEY, HOW DO YOU DO THAT?

I'M NOT THE ONLY ONE WHO HAS CONNECTIONS TO THE RECORDS. COME LOOK AT THIS.

LOOK, ITS A CHECK AND ANOTHER LITTLE MAN!

I WORK FOR THE SECRETARY OF STATE, WILLIAM SEWARD.

POP!

I WAS IN THE ROOM WHEN THIS CHECK TO BUY ALASKA WAS SIGNED. SOME PEOPLE THINK IT'S CRAZY, BUT SECRETARY SEWARD THINKS THIS IS AN IMPORTANT OPPORTUNITY TO EXPAND THE UNITED STATES.

ZIP!

I KNOW ABOUT THIS! I KNOW ALL SORTS OF STUFF ABOUT ALASKA. LIKE THE ARCTIC NATIONAL WILDLIFE REFUGE, HOW BIG IT IS, WHAT KIND OF PLANTS AND ANIMALS LIVE THERE...I EXCHANGE EMAILS WITH A FRIEND WHO LIVES THERE.

I GUESS I KNEW THE U.S. BOUGHT ALASKA, BUT I NEVER THOUGHT THERE'D BE AN ACTUAL CHECK. OR THAT ANYONE WOULD KEEP IT. HOW MUCH IS IT FOR, ANYWAY?

7.2 MILLION. IT SOUNDS LIKE A LOT, BUT ACTUALLY FOR ABOUT 2 CENTS AN ACRE, OUR COUNTRY GOT AN AREA TWICE THE SIZE OF TEXAS!

WOW, YOU DO KNOW A LOT ABOUT THIS.

IF I USE THE WATCH, WILL IT TAKE US SOMEWHERE?

SURE.

WHAT IS THIS?

I'M A NEWSIE! I SELL NEWSPAPERS.

SOMETIMES I WORK FROM BEFORE SUNUP. UNTIL AFTER MIDNIGHT! I'M 11, I THINK. MOST OF THE BOYS WITH ME ARE YOUNGER. WE WORK OUTSIDE NO MATTER WHAT THE WEATHER. NO SALES, NO PAY. THIS GUY CAME AROUND. TOOK OUR PICTURE. ASKED US A BUNCH OF QUESTIONS, TOO. HEY! GOTTA GET BACK TO WORK!

ZIP!

I KNOW THIS PHOTO, LEWIS HINE TOOK IT. HE TOOK LOTS OF PHOTOS OF KIDS WORKING. KIDS USED TO WORK LONG HOURS FOR ALMOST NO PAY.

IT WAS LEGAL FOR KIDS THAT YOUNG TO WORK? IT'S NOT NOW-- THEY'D HAVE TO BE IN SCHOOL!

THAT'S RIGHT. THESE PHOTOS ARE PART OF THE REASON THINGS CHANGED. PEOPLE USED THE PHOTOS TO SHOW WHAT WAS HAPPENING TO THESE CHILDREN. THIS PROOF HELPED MOVE OUR GOVERNMENT TO CHANGE LAWS-- AND THAT CHANGED PEOPLE'S LIVES.

DO YOU STILL THINK THIS IS JUST OLD BORING STUFF?

WELL, SURE, THE FOUR THINGS YOU SHOWED US WERE SORT OF INTERESTING, BUT I'M NOT SURE IT REALLY CONNECTS TO MY LIFE.

I MEAN, ITS OKAY FOR HER, SHE LOVES HISTORY! BUT I DON'T.

I THINK YOU NEED ONE MORE RECORD, THEN.

TO BE CONTINUED...

29

WOW! MORE COOL STUFF

This passenger arrival list and declaration of intention are records of immigration to the United States. Immigration has been an important part of the American story.

August 19, 1981

...use,

...States.

I nominate Sandra Day O'Connor, of Arizona, to be

an Associate Justice of the Supreme Court of the United States,

vice Potter Stewart, retired.

Ronald Reagan

This is President Ronald Reagan's nomination of Sandra Day O'Connor to the Supreme Court. She was the first female justice to sit on the Supreme Court.

DECLARATION OF INTENTION
(Invalid for all purposes seven years after the date hereof)

United States of America — District
District of New Jersey : ss: of The United States at Trenton

I, Dr. Albert Einstein
now residing at 112 Mercer St., Princeton, Mercer, N.J.
occupation Professor, aged 56 years, do declare on oath that my personal description is:
Sex Male, color White, complexion Fair, color of eyes Brown,
color of hair Grey, height 5 feet 7 inches; weight 175 pounds; visible distinctive marks none
race Hebrew; nationality German
I was born in Ulm, Germany, on March 14, 1879
I am married. The name of my wife is Elsa; she or he was
born at Hechingen, Germany, on January 18, 1876, entered the United States
at New York, N.Y., on June 5, 1935, for permanent residence therein, and now
resides at with me. I have 2 children, and the name, date and place of birth,
and place of residence of each of said children are as follows: Albert born 5-14-1905 and
Eduard born 6-28-1910 both born and reside in Switzerland

I have not heretofore made a declaration of intention: Number ____, on ____
at ____
my last foreign residence was Bermuda, Great Britain
I emigrated to the United States of America from Bermuda, Great Britain
my lawful entry for permanent residence in the United States was at New York, N.Y.,
under the name of Albert Einstein, on June 3, 1935,
on the vessel SS Queen of Bermuda

I will, before being admitted to citizenship, renounce forever all allegiance and fidelity to any foreign prince, potentate, state, or sovereignty, and particularly, by name, to the prince, potentate, state, or sovereignty of which I may be at the time of admission a citizen or subject; I am not an anarchist; I am not a polygamist nor a believer in the practice of polygamy; and it is my intention in good faith to become a citizen of the United States of America and to reside permanently therein; and I certify that the photograph affixed to the duplicate and triplicate hereof is a likeness of me: So HELP ME GOD.

Albert Einstein

Subscribed and sworn to before me in the office of the Clerk of said Court,
at Trenton, N.J., this 15th day of January
anno Domini 1936. Certification No. 3-120742 from the Commissioner of Immigration and Naturalization showing the lawful entry of the declarant for permanent residence on the date stated above, has been received by me. The photograph affixed to the duplicate and triplicate hereof is a likeness of the declarant.

George T. Cranmer
[SEAL] Clerk of the U.S. District Court.
By ____, Deputy Clerk.

No. 5773

(The seal of the court will be impressed so as to cover a portion of the photograph.)

Form 2202—L-A
U.S. DEPARTMENT OF LABOR
IMMIGRATION AND NATURALIZATION SERVICE

30

Our NUMBERS are HUGE!

It's hard to imagine just exactly how much stuff we have loaded into the Archives already. It can make your head spin just thinking about it — but that's what makes us one powerful resource for our Archivists-in-Training. Check this out . . .

How Many Pages?

There are **800,000 cubic feet** of storage at the main building of the National Archives Building in Washington, DC.

If one cubic foot = 2500 pages, how many pages are stored there?

How Much Time?

There are about **3,000,000 feet** of film footage in the National Archives. Assume half of the film is 16mm and half is 35mm. It takes 11 minutes to watch 400 feet of 16mm film. It takes 11 minutes to watch 1000 feet of 35mm film.

How long would it take you to watch all the film in the National Archives? How many minutes? How many hours? How many days?

How Long?

The National Archives at College Park, MD, contains **520 miles** of shelving.

If it took you 30 seconds to place documents onto one running foot of shelving, how long would it take you to fill the entire building?

How Long? If you worked 8 hours a day, 5 days a week, and never took vacation, it would take 11 years to fill the building!

How Much Time? It would take 57,750 minutes, or 962.5 hours, or 40 days to watch all of the film.

Answers: How Many Pages? The main building holds about 2,000,000,000 (2 billion) pages!

31

Archivist-in-Training Alert:
We May Be Closer Than You Think!

The National Archives and Records Administration (NARA) is not one place, but actually a network of over thirty facilities across the country. As an Archivist-in-Training, you need to know where these facilities are — in case you get called in for duty. So…

- Look at the map.
- Which facility is closest to you?

National Archives

⭐ *Regional Facilities*

⭐ *Presidential Libraries*

NOW GO TO WWW.ARCHIVES.GOV
to find the location of the Archives facility closest to you.

Try To Find Us!

The virtual Archives are just a few clicks away!

Can't visit us when you need something? No worries! The National Archives is also online, so you can do research from home, school, or the library. We're just a few clicks away.

CHECK US OUT!

Go to *www.archives.gov/research/arc/*. Click the button in the upper left labeled "search." That will take you to a new page, called ARC Basic Search. (ARC is the Archival Research Catalog.) There you can type key words to do searches.

Try doing key word searches on

- Your town
- Your county
- Your state

What do you find? What kinds of information are available? What else might you want to look for?

WWW.ARCHIVES.GOV

Although every year we add more records online from the billions of films, documents, audio recordings, and photographs we hold, not all National Archives records go to the web. Online is a great place to start your research, but for a real Archivist-in-Training, nothing will replace a visit to an Archives facility!

EVEN MORE COOL STUFF

Views of the unsettled 19th-century west: A covered wagon crosses the Nebraska plains and a painting of an Oregon Territory valley shows the boundary with Canada.

№ 43.391.

ORESTES CLEVELAND.

PENCILS.

CLASSIFICATION 43391 DIVISION.

Patented July. 5. 1864.

New inventions, even for something as simple as a pencil, require a detailed drawing!

Richard H. Taylor

Wm Kemble Hall

Orestes Cleveland

INVENTOR

ENGINEER AND COUNSEL IN PATENT CASES.

169 Broadway, New York.

Native Americans appear in National Archives records in a variety of ways — like this World War II photograph of Navajo code talkers and this 1807 treaty between the U.S. and the Ottawa, Chippewa, Wyandot, and Potawatomi tribes.

**U. S. NAVAL AIR STATION, KODIAK, ALASKA
NAVAL COMMUNICATIONS**

Heading   NPG NR 63 F L Z F5L 071830 C8Q TART O BT

From: CINCPAC   Date   7 DEC 41

To: ALL SHIPS PRESENT AT HAWAIIN AREA.

Info: - U R G E N T -

DEFERRED unless otherwise checked | ROUTINE.......... | PRIORIT

AIRRAID ON REARLHARBOR X THIS IS NO DRILL

This camera—owned by Mr. Abraham Zapruder—recorded the only complete film record of President John F. Kennedy's assassination.

Records of war: An urgent telegram—what has happened? Women join the Marine Corps. A Marine soldier lands at Danang, Vietnam.

FAD | NRAB | OOD | WDO

My Experience...

Okay, Archivist-in-Training, now it's YOUR turn to collect records of an event — your visit to the National Archives.

You can SAY you went to the National Archives, but can you PROVE it? That's why even little scraps of documentation are important. (Like that gift store receipt you just stuffed in your pocket that might get mangled in the washer!) Add 'em up and they'll tell a story — YOUR story. Record what you can track down in the spaces below. If you can, put the documents in the back pocket of this book!

WHAT RECORDS CAN YOU USE TO DOCUMENT...

What *kinds* of records of your visit do you have?

- Photos?
- Postcards?
- Ticket stubs?
- Books?
- Brochures?
- Something from the gift store?

which National Archives facility you visited?

how you traveled there?

what you saw?

Did you know that anyone over the age of fourteen with valid photo identification can conduct research in any National Archives facilities?

Every day, government agencies create mounds of new records. Only the lucky ones get transferred to the National Archives.

what you remember the most?

what you liked the best?

Planning a trip to the National Archives?

AiT Members are good at advance planning. Get ready BEFORE you go, so you don't come back empty-handed from your mission!

- **What kinds of records of my visit do I want to collect?**

- **What will help me remember my visit?**

- **What will help me show my visit to others?**

AiT Hint: You might want to check out www.archives.gov to scout out the place and pull your plan together!

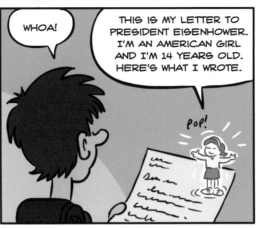

WHOA!

THIS IS MY LETTER TO PRESIDENT EISENHOWER. I'M AN AMERICAN GIRL AND I'M 14 YEARS OLD. HERE'S WHAT I WROTE.

I'M CRUSHED THAT YOU'RE MAKING ELVIS PRESLEY JOIN THE ARMY! YOU DON'T UNDERSTAND WHAT HE MEANS TO US! IT'S JUST SELFISH, THAT'S WHAT IT IS. DON'T TAKE HIM AWAY FROM US!

SHE CERTAINLY GAVE HIM A PIECE OF HER MIND! I REMEMBER MY GRANDMA LOVED ELVIS, TOO.

YEAH, SHE KIND OF REMINDS ME OF MY GRANDMOTHER. NOT 'CAUSE OF ELVIS, BUT THE LETTER WRITING. SHE WAS ALWAYS WRITING LETTERS TO THE GOVERNMENT.

IS THAT MY GRANDMOTHER? *THAT IS MY GRANDMOTHER!* SHE WAS AN ELVIS FAN? AND SHE WROTE TO THE PRESIDENT ABOUT IT??

YES. AND SHE BECAME A FAN OF WRITING HER GOVERNMENT, TOO. THAT WAS HER FIRST LETTER TO THE PRESIDENT, BUT DEFINITELY NOT HER LAST. YOU'RE RIGHT, SHE KEPT WRITING ABOUT ALL SORTS OF THINGS. I WONDER IF THE PRESIDENT EVER ANSWERED HER.

HOW DID THIS LETTER END UP *HERE?*

EVERY YEAR, AMERICAN CITIZENS SEND MILLIONS OF LETTERS TO THEIR GOVERNMENT OFFICIALS. WE KEEP 'EM...NOT ALL OF THEM, BUT LOTS OF THEM. THEY ARE AN EXPRESSION OF PEOPLE'S CONNECTION WITH THEIR GOVERNMENT.

IT'S SORT OF LIKE I'M IN THE NATIONAL ARCHIVES.

FAMILIES, FRIENDS, LEADERS, PROTECTORS... WE'RE ALL IN HERE, AREN'T WE?

AND WHO KNOWS JUST HOW YOU TWO WILL GET ADDED SOME DAY? THERE'S PLENTY OF TIME. AND SPEAKING OF TIME...

HEY, WE'RE BACK!

BUT LOOK. NO TIME HAS PASSED!

BUT WE WERE IN THERE FOR HOURS!

I KNOW, BUT LOOK AROUND.

AN HOUR LATER...

HERE, MISS, YOU DROPPED THIS.

OH, THANKS...

HELLO, MOM?

HEY! WE JUST FINISHED CLEANING OUT THE GARAGE. SO GOOD TO THROW AWAY ALL THAT OLD JUNK FROM YOUR GRANDMA. OUT IT GOES... MORE ROOM FOR THE CAR!

WAIT, YOU CAN'T JUST THROW IT ALL OUT! THERE MIGHT BE SOMETHING IMPORTANT IN THERE! OR INTERESTING...AT LEAST WAIT UNTIL I GET HOME, SO WE CAN DECIDE WHAT TO SAVE.

WHERE ARE YOU GOING TO KEEP ALL THAT JUNK?

I'LL FIGURE IT OUT. THEY'RE RECORDS, NOT JUNK!

THAT WAS MY MOM... YOU WOULDN'T BELIEVE IT! THEY'RE TOSSING OUT ALL MY GRANDMA'S STUFF FROM THE GARAGE!

YIKES!

UMMM, MAYBE YOU COULD... YOU KNOW... COME BY MY HOUSE TOMORROW AND LOOK OVER THE STUFF MY PARENTS WERE GONNA THROW OUT.

MAYBE THERE WILL EVEN BE AN ANSWER FROM PRESIDENT EISENHOWER! WOULDN'T THAT BE AMAZING?

WELL, I GUESS YOU'LL NEED THIS, THEN.

National Archives' Archivist-in-Training
MEMBER
This is to certify that
is an Archivist-in-Training since

HUH? WHERE DID MY AIT CARD COME FROM?

WELL, YOU HAVE INSIDE CONNECTIONS AT THE ARCHIVES NOW!

END

NOW IT'S YOUR TURN TO CONNECT TO THE NATIONAL ARCHIVES. THE RECORDS ARE WAITING FOR YOU -- COME AND DISCOVER YOUR STORIES! AND AS YOU RESEARCH, KEEP TRACK OF WHERE YOU FOUND RECORDS. SEE THE BACK COVER FOR MORE ABOUT THIS IMPORTANT PART OF RESEARCHING.

Congrats—you did it! By completing this training kit, you're now an official Archivist-in-Training. But the training doesn't stop here. Take your Membership Card from the next page, fill it out, and keep exploring the National Archives. Share what you find. Spread the word—and help us protect and learn from this national treasure!

Many thanks,
Allen Weinstein
Archivist of the United States

Member File Marker

THE NATIONAL ARCHIVES'
ARCHIVIST·IN·TRAINING

We the Archivists-in-Training

find, save, and share records that help us to better understand the past.

MEMBER

National Archives' Archivist-in-Training

This is to certify that ....

is an Archivist-in-Training since .... , 20 ....

Put your RECORDS here!

Did you see where my filing cabinets went?

I archived them.